FISH·CARVING Basics

Volume Two

HOW TO PAINT

Volume Two

HOW TO PAINT

Curtis J. Badger

STACKPOLE
BOOKS

Published by
STACKPOLE BOOKS
5067 Ritter Road
Mechanicsburg, PA 17055

Printed in Hong Kong

10 9 8 7 6 5 4 3 2 1

First edition

Cover design by Caroline Miller

Interior design by Marcia Lee Dobbs

Library of Congress Cataloging-in-Publication Data
(Revised for vol. 2)

Badger, Curtis J.
     Fish carving basics.

     Contents: v. 1. How to carve.—v. 2. How to paint.
     1. Wood-carving—Technique.   2. Fishes in art.
3. Painting—Technique.   I. Title.
TT199.7.B335   1994   731'.832   93-30588
ISBN 0-8117-2524-3 (v. 1)
ISBN 0-8117-2440-9 (v. 2)

Contents

Foreword

After featuring the carving skills of Earl Federine, Dave Johnson, and Bob Swain in volume 1 of the Fish Carving Basics series, it seemed only natural to follow up with a book on painting. After all, it just didn't seem fair to whet the reader's appetite with specific projects and not follow up on them.

Earl, Dave, and Bob all have very different approaches to carving and painting, so by taking a look at their painting techniques you will learn several different options. Earl demonstrates his airbrush technique, Dave applies acrylic paint with brushes, and Bob creates an aged look using Japan paints.

Again, I'd like to thank all three artists for allowing me to look over their shoulders with the camera. It's always exciting to see a raw piece of wood transformed into a beautiful finished item that will be enjoyed for years to come.

1
Earl Federine

Airbrushing a Redfish with

When painting a redfish, research is very important, especially field research. "Redfish vary in color depending upon where they live," Earl Federine explains. "Fish along the coastal waters are lighter in color than those we have here in the Louisiana bayou country, where the water is brackish."

To prove the point, Earl suggested that we catch a few fish and check out their colors. So we loaded some fishing tackle into Earl's boat and headed out for the marshes near Grand Isle, not far from Earl's home in Cut Off. The marshes are private, but Earl has a lease, and his friend Ted St. Pierre has a camp in a marsh rich with redfish.

In a shallow pond we could see the subtle wake of a red as it chased shrimp and minnows. We tied on lures—Earl a buzzbait and I a golden Johnson spoon—and in short order we were up to our elbows in field research.

Observation one: A 5-pound redfish, when hooked on light tackle in a foot of water, closely resembles a torpedo whose navigational system has gone bonkers: The fish goes to the left, goes to the right, comes to the boat, goes under the boat, circles, and splashes. Finally Earl nets it.

Observation two: The back of the fish is a dusky bronze, but there are all sorts of tricky color variations depending on how the light hits the fish. Earl points out a subtle band of iridescent blue around the tail fin. I hadn't noticed that before. See how important field research is?

More work is called for. So that we can determine the variations in color among many different fish, we continue until we have our legal limit of six fish each.

Observation three: Ah, yes. Some fish are darker than others, some have more red or bronze. On some the blue line along the tail is more prominent. On larger ones there are bronze splotches on the scales along the sides.

We deduce that when painting a redfish, a certain degree of artistic license is called for. There is no secret formula, no single correct color. A paint-by-number project this is not.

Back at the laboratory, field research completed, Earl assembles his arsenal of paints. He uses lacquers, the same stuff that's on my Ford pickup. While the redfish is not exactly a gaudy tropical specimen, it requires a remarkable palette of colors. There are something like ten bottles of paint: white and pearl silver for the belly; vivid orange, bronze, brown, and gold pearl for the back; black and iridescent blue for detailing; red for the gills; and yellow or gold for the inside of the mouth.

Earl uses an airbrush, which is very handy for painting a redfish because the airbrush makes it easy to blend and overlap colors. The redfish is not a single color but a series of colors, one laid over the other. If you do it right, one color will show through another,

Earl uses lacquer paints similar to those used in vehicle paint shops. The paints are diluted with thinner, and a retardant is used to slow the drying time if necessary. Earl uses ten different colors to paint the redfish. "When you look at the fish you can get the impression that it's just bronze and white, but there are actually a lot of different shades that you need to capture," he says. The lacquer paints can be purchased from carving supply or taxidermy shops.

giving the illusion of depth and richness. The airbrush is good for this because it applies a fine mist of paint, and Earl can spray on many applications without worrying about blocking up carved detail such as scales and fins.

This redfish is the one Earl carved in volume 1 of this series. It's part of a composition Earl is making as a Christmas gift for his friend Ted St. Pierre, whose camp we used when conducting field research. So merry Christmas, Ted; it couldn't have been done without you.

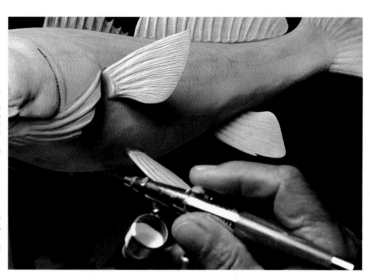

Before painting, Earl first seals the wood surface by brushing on Tee-Kay's Rapid Dry Wood Sealer, available from Curt's Waterfowl Corner (Box 228, Montegut, LA 70377). He then applies a coat of Polytranspar white lacquer with the airbrush.

Earl paints the belly of the fish with a white base coat, feathering the edges along the sides where the white will be blended with the bronze color. The white will later be painted with pearl silver.

Earl paints the right side of the fish with white.
The stand, which is Earl's design, enables him to
paint all areas of the fish without handling it, as
oils from the skin can prevent paint from adhering
properly. The point where the fish is attached to
the stand will serve as the mounting point when
Earl attaches the fish to a driftwood background.

The fins, as well as the body of the fish, are painted white. Earl experiments with the flow of the paint to get a good spray. If the paint dries too soon, retarder can be added. Paint is diluted with thinner at approximately a 2:1 ratio. "The point is to get a good spray," Earl says. "If you have it too thin, you just have to apply a little more."

Earl cleans his airbrush with thinner, often
spraying the fish with the diluted paint. "It's not
thick enough to cover detail, but it adds a bit more
color." Before going to the red color, Earl sprays
some #972 pearl silver over the white. This dulls
the white somewhat and adds luster.

The bronze back of the redfish gets a base coat of #801 vivid orange, a surprisingly bright color considering the more muted tone of the finish. But the orange base will help create the illusion of depth. Again, the paint is diluted with thinner. Earl begins by painting the dorsal fins and the head. He holds the brush at an angle to the spines, causing paint to build up on them while being applied more thinly on the connecting tissues between the spines.

The vivid orange color overlaps the white along the sides of the fish. The advantage of the airbrush in this case is that it allows a gradual transition between the colors. "You can do the blending so much easier," Earl notes.

Earl applies vivid orange to the top of the fish, making the color deeper there and allowing the overspray to create a gradual edge. Earl began using the airbrush when he was doing taxidermy work and later adapted it to carving.

A close-up shows the detail around the head of the fish. Notice the soft edge where the orange blends with the white. Also note the application of orange around the fish's mouth.

The dorsal fins and the back of the fish have a heavier application of color than do the sides. The airbrush makes this transition area easy to achieve. "At this point, it looks like we've got a beautiful tropical fish," Earl says.

The orange will be toned down with an application of #933 bronze metallic paint applied to the back. The overspray creates a soft transition along the sides, allowing some of the orange to show through.

A small amount of bronze is applied to the pectoral and pelvic fins. A piece of cardboard shields the body of the fish from the spray.

Earl now applies gold pearl to the back, again letting it overlap onto the orange and white transition area on the sides. The overlapping colors create an illusion of depth, and as with a real fish, the colors change slightly as the light striking the fish and the angle of view change.

The head of the fish with applications of orange,
bronze, white, white pearl, and gold pearl. Painting
a redfish is not an exact science, Earl says,
because the fish vary in color depending on their
surroundings. On the East Coast, redfish are
known as channel bass or red drum and are much
whiter than their cousins found in the more
brackish waters of Bayou Lafourche. So some
artistic license is allowed.

Detail of the side and back shows the effect of blending colors with the airbrush. Notice, too, how Earl made the dorsal spines a more golden color than the tissue that separates them. He did this by holding the airbrush at a sharp angle to the spines, which allowed more paint to fall on them.

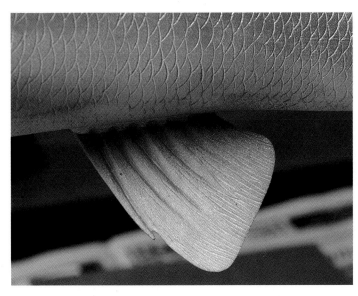

A little bronze and some gold pearl add luster to the lower fins, such as the pelvic fin shown here.

The top of the fish, including the dorsal fins, will be darkened by an application of #203 brown. The spray is directed downward from the top of the fish. The back and dorsal fins get most of the color, with a small amount falling onto the sides and lower fins.

The application of brown has darkened the back of the fish, and it has also emphasized carved detail such as the spines, scales, and lateral line.

Earl at work in his studio in Cut Off. In the background is the taxidermy mount Earl uses for reference in carving and painting the fish.

Notice the blending of colors on the head and gill covers of the fish, a combination of the original application of white, vivid orange, bronze, and brown. The glass eye is painted over and will be cleaned when the painting is completed.

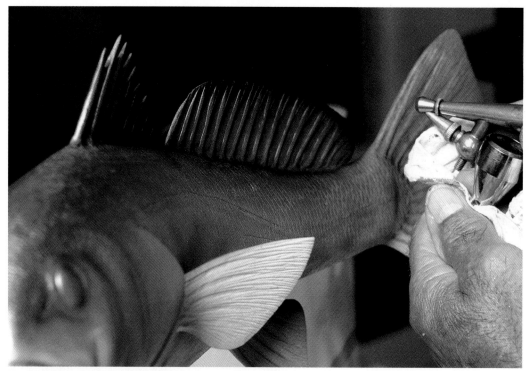

To further darken the back of the fish and to add accents, Earl loads some #601 black into the cup and sprays the tops of the dorsal fins.

"Sometimes the brown is enough to add accents, but I usually like to add a little black, especially along the dorsal fins to emphasize detail," Earl explains.

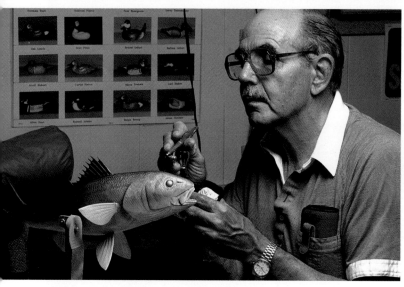

The black is also used to shade the tail, the top of the fish where the dorsals meet the body, and along the top of the head.

A piece of cardboard shields the body of the fish as Earl applies a light coat of #931 iridescent gold to the pelvic and pectoral fins.

Gold also is applied to the back of the fish to lighten it slightly. Painting this area is often a matter of fine-tuning: Brown and black will darken it, but if it becomes too dark, a mist of iridescent gold will lighten it.

Earl applies gold to the face of the fish, blending it into the reddish brown areas of the mouth.

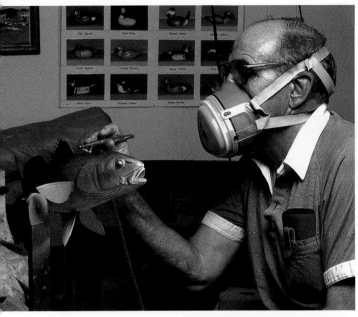

Lacquer should be applied in a well-ventilated area. Earl uses several exhaust fans when he paints, and he often will use a mask. This one was purchased from an auto body shop.

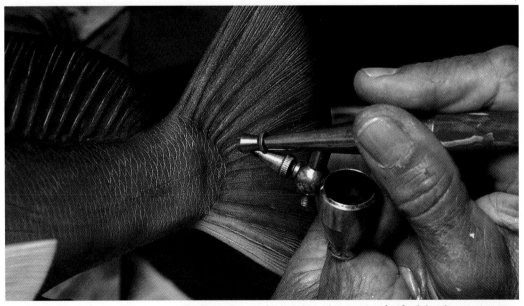

Before he paints the characteristic black spot near the tail of the redfish, Earl first lightens the area around it with an application of iridescent gold. By applying first the gold, then the black, Earl will create a slight halo around the spot.

The black is now applied to the center of the gold spot, leaving a soft edge.

Earl gradually enlarges the spot, leaving a soft ring of gold around it. Redfish often have more than one spot, and the locations vary.

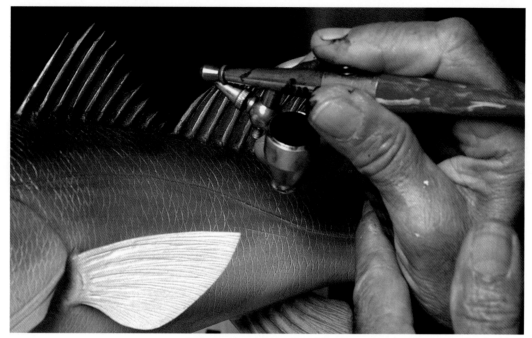

While Earl has the black paint in the cup, he decides to darken the dorsal fins a bit more, toning down the gold.

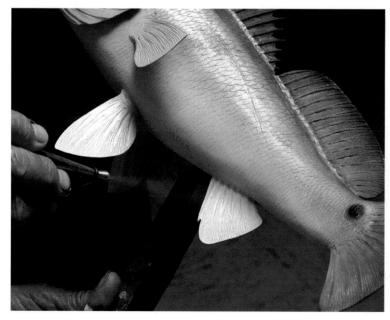

Although Earl painted the belly and lower fins white early in the project, these areas now need to be touched up because they were darkened by overspray. Earl lightens the pelvic fin here.

The area around the pectoral fin is lightened,
with the white blended into the darker areas along
the side of the fish.

Finally, Earl applies
white to the mouth
area and the lower
jaw.

Earl decides that the fins are too light and wants to give them more color. A thin application of vivid orange, followed by iridescent gold, does the trick.

Earl applied orange to the right pectoral fin, and now he goes over it with gold, shielding the fish with cardboard. With the airbrush the mist of color is so thin that repeated applications can be made to adjust the color without blocking up the carved detail.

"When you catch a live fish, you can hold it up to the light and see a thin line of iridescent blue along the edge of the tail fin," Earl says. He paints the edge of the tail black, then adds iridescent blue along the perimeter.

The belly of the fish gets an application of pearl silver, which mutes the white somewhat and adds a slight luster.

The inside of the mouth can be painted with a very light application of gold or bright yellow. The paint job is nearly complete, and Earl has used a knife to scrape the paint from the glass eye.

Earl decides the back is a bit too light, so he finishes with a final application of brown. A clear lacquer spray adds a glossy, wet look to the fish.

This close-up shows detail of the head and eye.

The finished redfish among some appropriate habitat: driftwood, shells, barnacles, and fishing lure.

2 Using Acrylics on a Butterfly Fish with Dave Johnson

The threadfin butterfly fish, a tropical saltwater species, is a favorite among fish carvers because of its bold design and bright colors. Dave Johnson carved the fish in volume 1 of this series, and now he demonstrates his painting technique.

Dave specializes in fish of the saltwater tropics, and the threadfin butterfly fish he does in this demonstration is typical of the species he enjoys doing. He carves and paints in a very realistic manner, researching both fish and habitat to ensure that both are presented correctly.

While Earl Federine used an airbrush loaded with lacquers to paint his redfish, Dave applies Liquitex brand acrylic paints with brushes. Either painting method will work; which one you should use depends on the project and on the technique you're most comfortable with. The airbrush is quicker and is easier for blending colors, especially on a large fish like the red. Of course, the equipment needed is fairly extensive, including an air compressor, a regulator, and the airbrush itself. When painting with acrylics, on the other hand, all you need are the paints, a sealer, brushes of varying sizes, and some water for diluting paints and for cleanup.

In painting the butterfly fish, Dave first uses airplane dope, a sanding sealer, to seal the surface of the wood and prevent the wood grain from rising. He then applies a base coat of titanium white. The fish shows varying degrees of yellow along the back and tail, and these are made with a mixture of Turner's yellow, cadmium yellow deep, and white.

Other colors Dave will use include Payne's gray, iridescent white, phthalo blue, raw umber, mars black, and burnt sienna. Spray varnish gives the fish a wet look.

"I have mixed feelings about giving a fish a glossy, wet look," Dave says. "If you take the fish out of the water, it's true that it does look like that, but underwater, in the fish's natural environment, it doesn't look glossy at all."

Dave usually will finish the fish with some degree of gloss and leave the surrounding habitat—coral, shells, and so on—with a flat finish.

Dave grew up in Montana and majored in marine biology at Westmont College in Santa Barbara, California, where he became interested in scuba diving. He now works in New Orleans as a corrosion engineer, a job that frequently takes him underwater. Dave's carving career began with waterfowl, but not surprisingly, his long-term interest in marine creatures eventually merged with his interest in carving. Ten years ago he switched to fish, and in 1986 he won the World Championship at the University of Kansas with a carving of a lionfish. His work is marketed through Dr. Ed Miller's Wildlife Unlimited Gallery, 2814 Bermuda Dunes, Missouri City, TX 77459.

Before beginning painting, Dave seals the surface of the wood with airplane dope diluted with thinner. This product, called Aero-Gloss, is available in hobby shops. "Airplane dope is basically a sanding sealer," Dave says, "and it keeps the wood grain from rising when you apply paint. If you thin it fifty-fifty it won't build up and obscure carved detail."

For carvers with an interest in tropical fish, Dave has recently produced a series of half-cast molded fish, which are handy for carving reference or painting practice. The series includes the four-eyed butterfly fish, the moorish idol, the copper-banded butterfly fish, the tri-colored angelfish or rock beauty, the sergeant major, and the blue tang. They are available for $15 each, which includes shipping, from Dave Johnson, P.O. Box 91, Belle Chasse, LA 70037.

Dave begins with the fins and covers the entire surface of the carving.

While the sealer dries, Dave prepares his first coat of paint. Liquitex titanium white will be used as a base coat, and here he uses a spray bottle to apply a fine mist of water to the paint, diluting it and preventing it from drying on the palette.

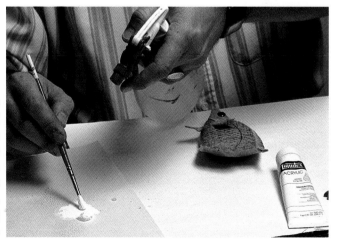

Dave brushes on the titanium white, beginning at the tail of the fish. He uses titanium white rather than gesso as a base coat because it is thinner and will not obscure fine detail such as small scales. On a larger fish without fine detail, he would use gesso as the base coat.

Dave dilutes the paint with water before applying it. He works it into the burned scale pattern. The white base coat is especially important when painting a light-colored fish such as this, because it makes the colors brighter and richer.

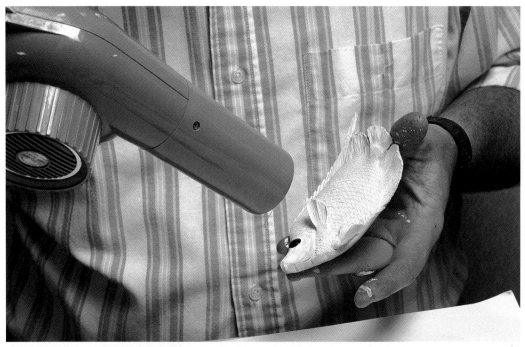

The paint can be dried with a hair dryer in only a minute or so, and then another coat can be applied.

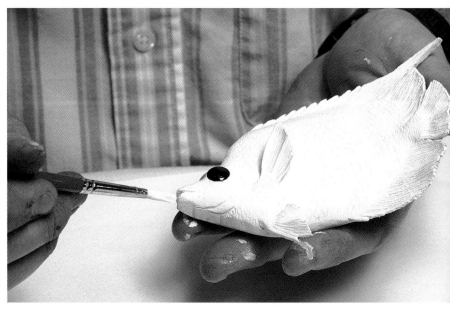

Dave applies enough washes of titanium white to get a uniform surface. The third thin coat has been put on, and the fish is now ready for some color. Dave advises using thin coats to avoid a buildup of paint in textured areas.

Dave uses books, photos, field guides, and if available, mounted fish as carving and painting reference. Colors vary from source to source, so some artistic license is called for. The reference photos, though, are vital in establishing color patterns and design. Dave photographs his finished work and uses the photos as reference when doing the same species again.

The color of the butterfly fish varies according to location, its age, and whether it is male or female, so there is no exact formula for the shade of yellow. Dave mixes a little cadmium yellow deep and Turner's yellow, then adds titanium white to get the value he wants.

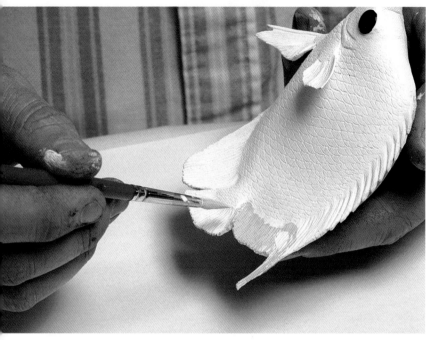

Dave begins by painting the outer edges of the second dorsals, and the caudal fin. The area where the black spot is located on the dorsal is not painted.

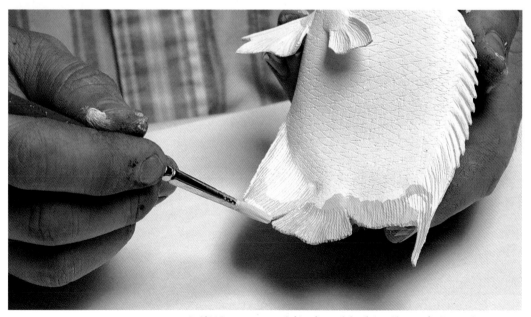

A little more white is added to the mixture to paint the pelvic fin. Dave blends the lighter yellow into the deeper color.

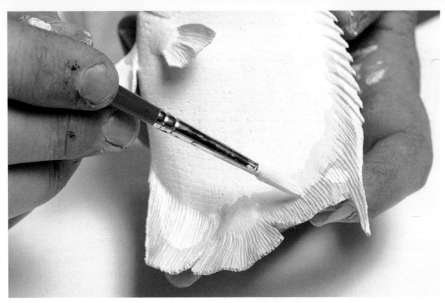

This lighter yellow is also used behind the deeper yellow on the caudal and dorsal fins.

Still more white is added to the paint mixture, and this third value of yellow is blended to the second one, as shown. The fish has a deep yellow tail, and the color gradually fades to white along the body.

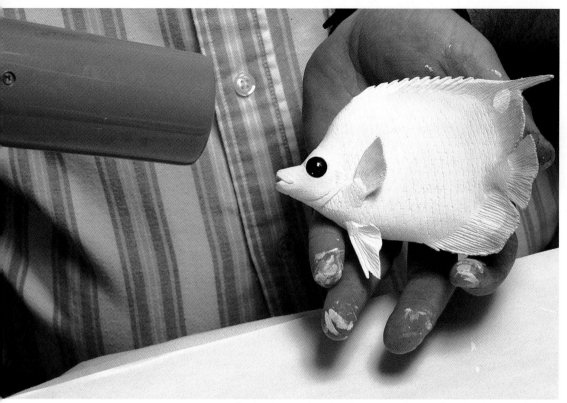

A hair dryer is used to dry the paint before going to the next step, adding white edges to the yellow fins. Note in this photo how the color is fairly intense on the tail, or caudal fin, and gradually fades to white.

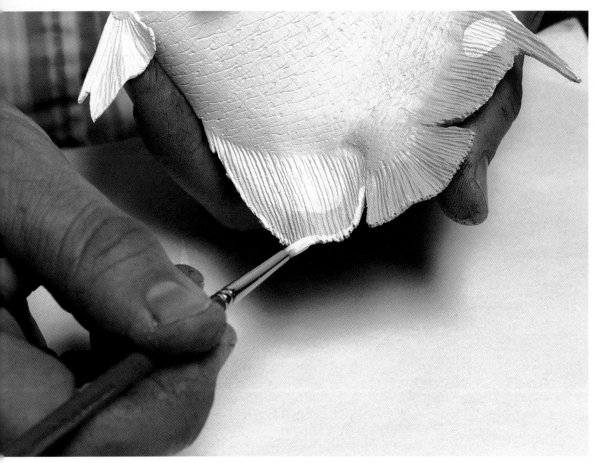

A small brush is used to touch up the areas that
need to be white again: the outer edges of the
caudal and anal fins, and the area where the black
spot will go.

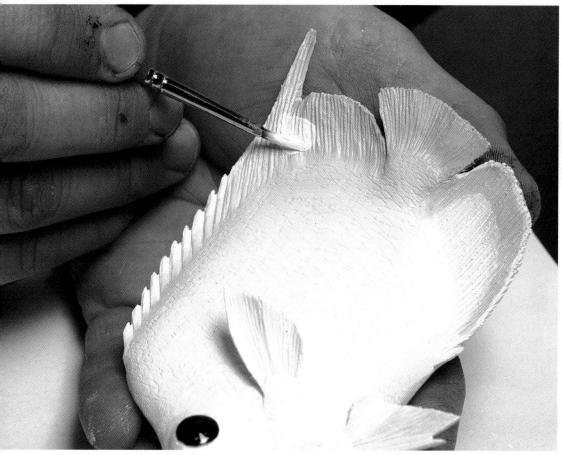

Dave redefines the area where the spot is located.
He paints it white because the black spot has a
faint white halo around it. When he applies the
black, he will leave a bit of white showing around
the perimeter.

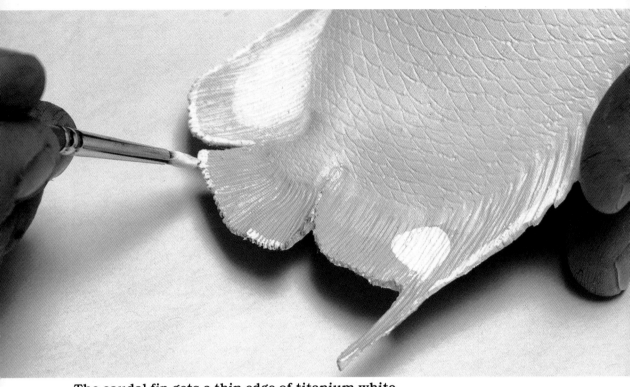

The caudal fin gets a thin edge of titanium white.
Note in this photo the shape of the area where the
black spot will be located. It's not round but is
shaped like a comma or a teardrop.

And now Dave is ready to paint the pelvic and pectoral fins, which are light gray. He mixes a little Payne's gray with the titanium white to get the value he wants.

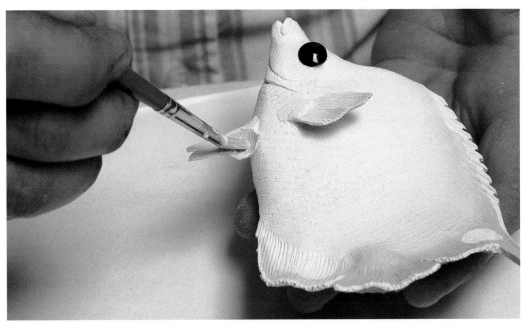

The Liquitex brand Payne's gray is bluish, a quality Dave likes about the color. Here he paints the pelvic fin.

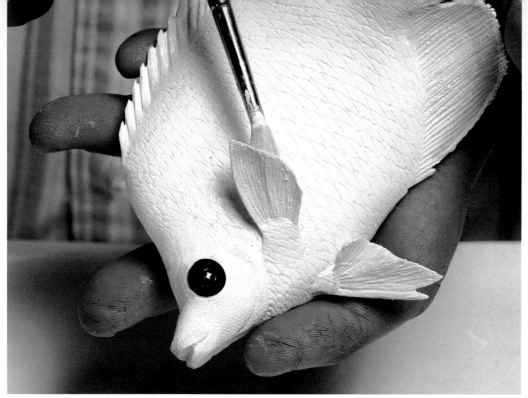

Don't forget to paint both sides of the fins, Dave warns. Here he paints the inside of the pectoral fin. Later, an application of iridescent white will give the fins a silvery, transparent quality.

Several values of gray go on the anal fin, beginning with a darker value against the yellow, followed by a lighter value, which gradually blends to white. Using Payne's gray and titanium white, Dave mixes several shades of gray.

The darker gray goes next to the yellow edge.

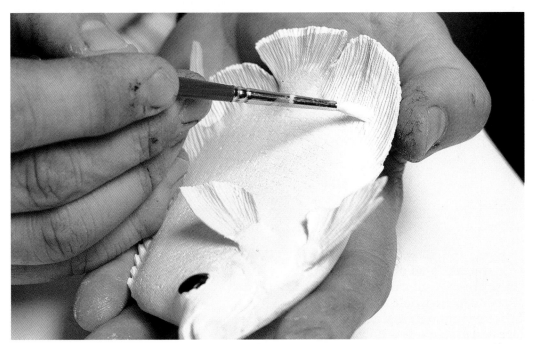

Dave then applies a lighter value of gray, blending the two together. Keeping the paints diluted with water helps in blending.

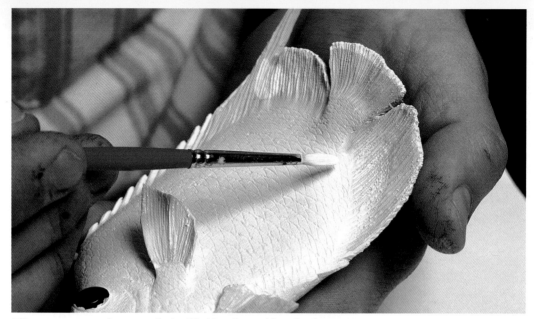

The gray area is complete. Notice how the darker
value of gray adjacent to the yellow gradually
fades to white.

Using his collection of reference
material, Dave prepares to paint
four yellow bands across the head
of the fish. He won't add the yellow
now but will instead paint the
areas white. Each yellow band has
a white edge, so Dave applies the
white background, blocking in the
bands.

The bands begin near the eye and extend across the forehead. Dave locates each with the application of titanium white. He will add the yellow stripes later.

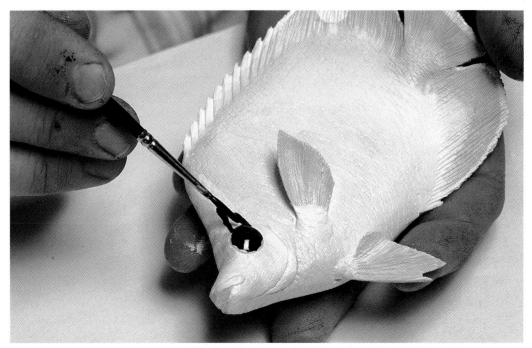

The bold eye stripe is painted with Payne's gray, straight from the tube. Dave uses his reference photos to determine the shape and dimensions of the stripe.

The stripe begins in front of the first dorsal fin and extends downward through the eye to the jaw, widening along the way.

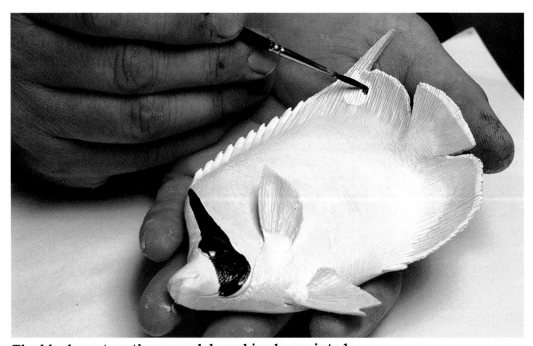

The black spot on the second dorsal is also painted with straight Payne's gray. It usually takes two or more applications to cover the white base coat, Dave notes.

Dave begins painting the spot in its center and moves toward the perimeter, following the general shape of the white outline.

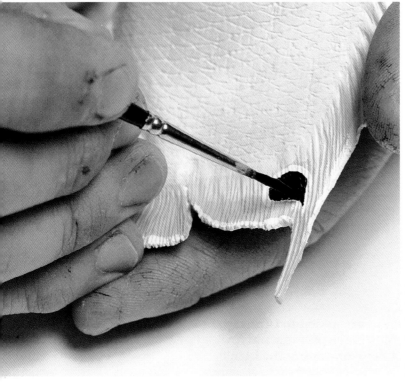

Dave wants to leave a thin white halo around the spot, so he is careful not to let the Payne's gray touch the yellow.

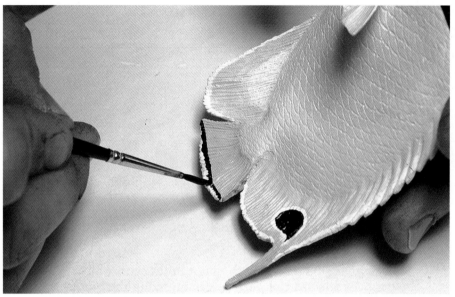

The fins get a thin edge of black, along with an edge of bluish gray. Dave uses straight Payne's gray here to paint the dark edge along the caudal fin.

Phthalo blue and some white are added to the gray to create this blue-gray color. Dave paints a narrow stripe on the edge of the tail, overlapping the black stripe somewhat.

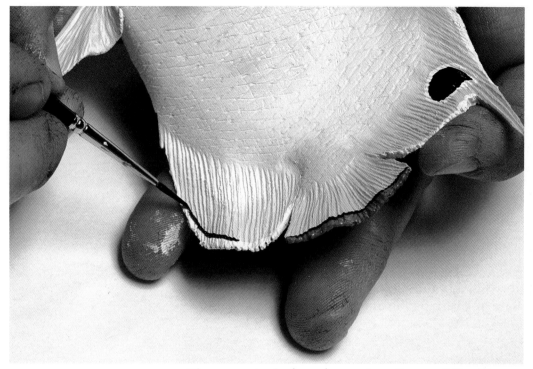

The same technique is used on the anal fin. The thin black stripe is applied using Payne's gray.

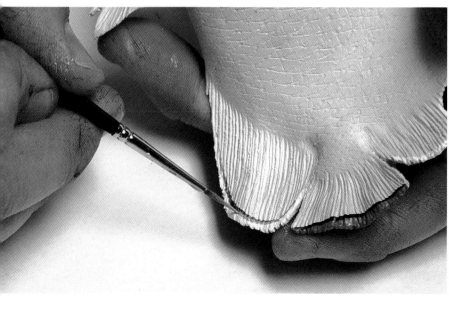

Phthalo blue, lightened with just a touch of titanium white, is used to paint the blue line.

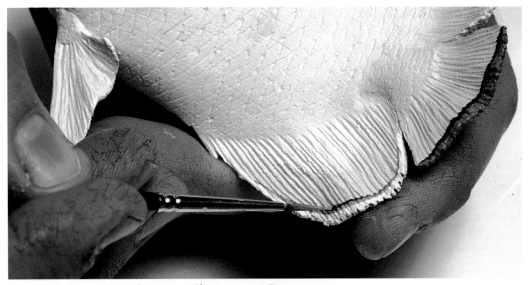

The fish has a lot of narrow lines, says Dave.
Here he overlaps the black line with the blue one,
making the black line even finer.

The lighter blue is applied over the darker value on
the caudal fin.

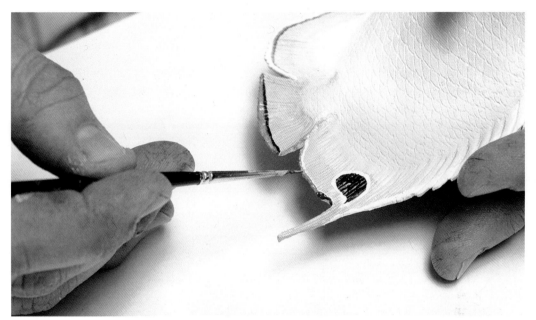

The lighter blue, made by mixing more white with the phthalo blue, is used to edge the lower part of the second dorsal.

A darker version of the same mix is used on the top part of the fin.

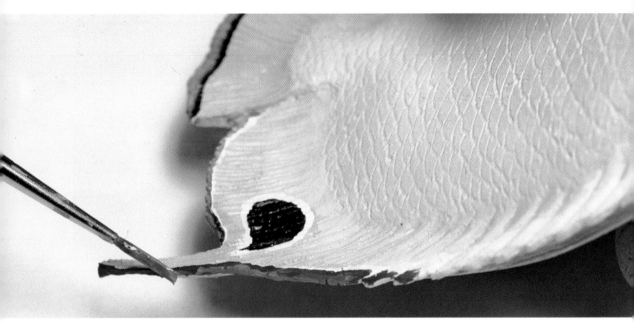

Dave then applies the lighter blue along the very
edge of this spine.

Dark blue can be added to the black on the dorsal
spot to give it a deeper, colder value.

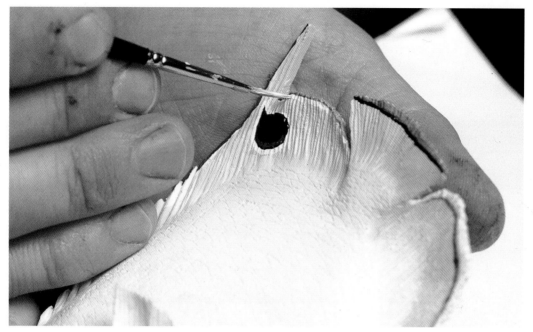

And now Dave will touch up the white lines along the dorsal fins, making the gray lines appear even finer. Here he uses straight titanium white with a very fine brush.

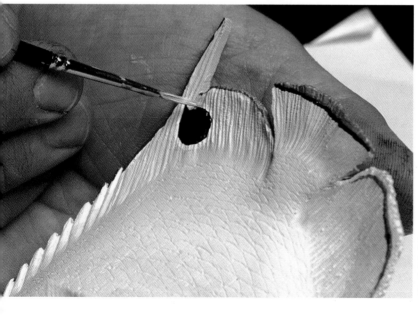

He uses the same paint to touch up the white halo around the dorsal spot.

The spines of the first dorsal are a light gray, made from titanium white tinted with Payne's gray. The tops of the spines are painted here.

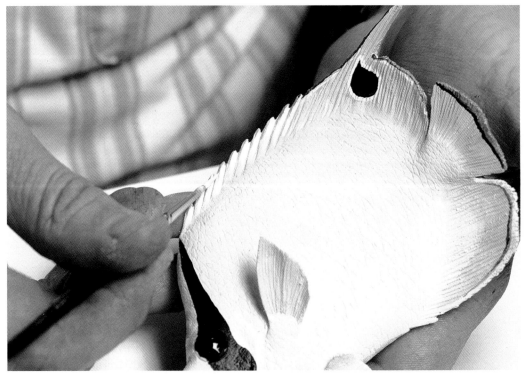

The areas between the spines are painted white.

Dave paints a white edge around the black eye stripe, refining its shape.

The four yellow stripes now go across the forehead, where Dave had painted the white lines earlier. Each yellow stripe goes on the white stripe, leaving a slight halo around it.

The butterfly fish has raw umber stripes of various values across its tail. Dave puts a dab of raw umber on the palette *(right),* along with mars black, Payne's gray, and titanium white. Turner's yellow, cadmium yellow deep, and phthalo blue are also shown.

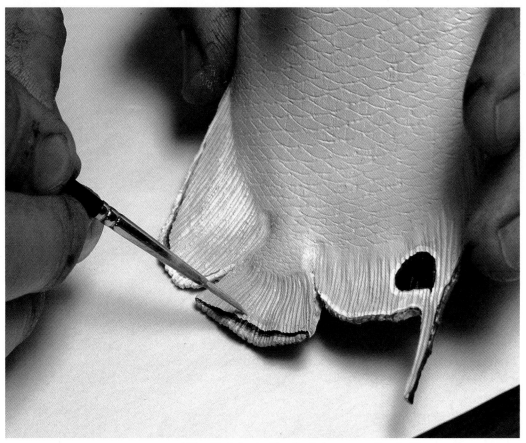

The light vertical stripes on the tail are a
combination of yellow, raw umber, and burnt
sienna. A single thin, yellowish line is sandwiched
between two darker ones. Dave begins here
with one of the darker outside lines, a mixture of
the three colors.

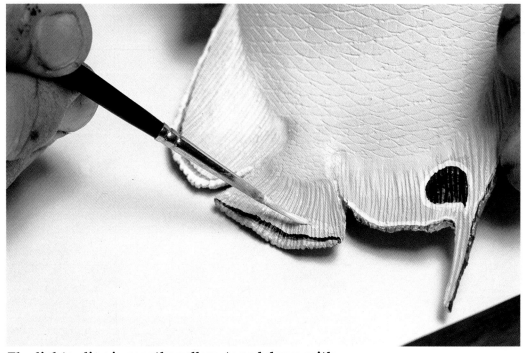

The lighter line is mostly yellow, toned down with a bit of white and burnt sienna.

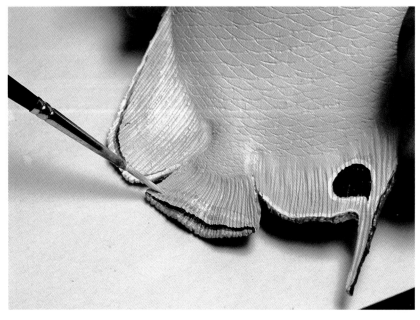

The stripe is finished with another application of the darker color.

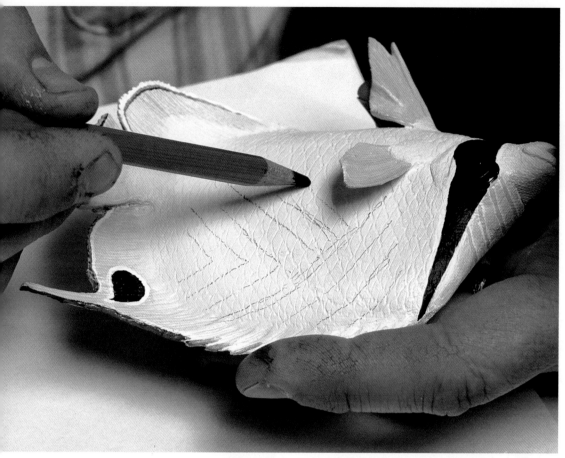

Dave is next going to paint the bold body stripes of the fish, but first he wants to consult his reference material and lightly sketch their position with a charcoal pencil.

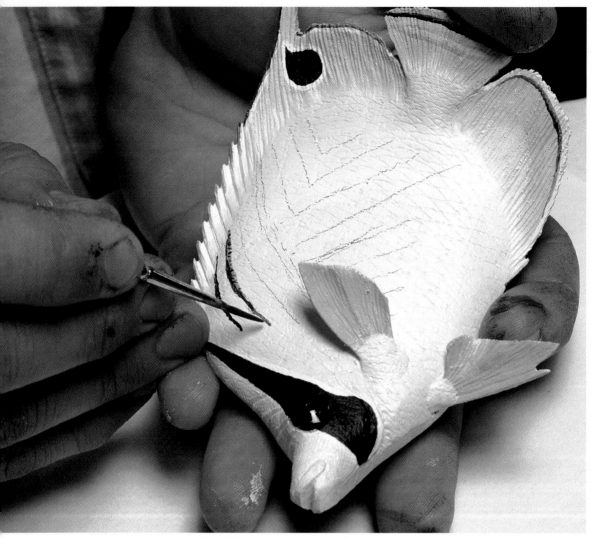

The lines are painted with raw umber and white.
Straight raw umber is used along the front part of
the fish, and white is added to the lines near the
tail where they gradually fade into the white and
yellow areas.

Dave adds more water to
the mixture to soften
the edges of the stripes.
Later, overall washes will
further reduce the
contrast.

Now Dave has added white to the mixture and is
blending the stripes into the tail.

"You don't want
the stripes to
be too stark,"
Dave cautions.
"They should
gradually fade
into the white
and yellow."

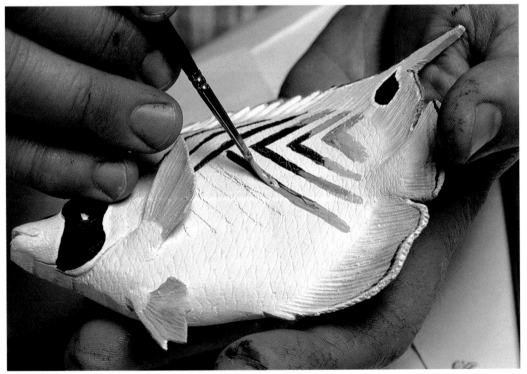

The lighter value of the color is painted adjacent
to, and overlapping, the darker values.

A little yellow and water can be added to form a thin wash of color, further blending the lines and the solid colors along the tail.

Dave uses white paint and moves the brush in a stippling motion along the edges of the darker stripes to soften them.

"You want to avoid hard lines," Dave advises.
"Soften them by stippling or by blending colors."
Note the difference between the softened lines
and those with the hard edge.

The sizes of the lines can be adjusted as the edges are softened. Dave re-defines the narrow stripes on the top part of the fish.

"It's often a matter of tinkering with it to get it the way you want it." Here Dave is softening the lines with gray to reduce the starkness.

Liquitex iridescent white is applied to the fins. "It's a pearl-type paint, and when you put it over white you get a silvery, transparent look," Dave says.

The pectoral and pelvic fins are painted, and now Dave dilutes the iridescent white with water and applies a thin wash to the top of the fish, where the stripes meet the dorsal area.

A thin wash of iridescence goes over the tail, where the stripes fade into white and yellow.

The forehead also gets an iridescent wash, toning it down.

Dave often will apply a very diluted wash of iridescent white over the entire scaled area of the fish, with the exception of the colored areas. The paint produces a silvery look when applied over white or gray, but it would dull areas like the eye stripe, which should remain bold, and the vivid yellow tail.

Undiluted iridescent white gives a bony look to the dorsal spines.

The butterfly fish is finished with an application
of Art Spray varnish, available at art-supply
dealers. The varnish gives a realistic wet look to
the fish and seals the colors.

3
Painting a Folk Art Fish
with Bob Swain

The redfish by Earl Federine and Dave Johnson's threadfin butterfly fish are realistic renderings with an emphasis on detail and accuracy. In this chapter, however, Bob Swain demonstrates that an attractive fish carving can be made using methods that are . . . well, not intended to fool anyone into thinking that the fish might actually be a taxidermy specimen.

Bob's methods are unorthodox, but they work. He applies paint and then sets it on fire. He adds fine detail, then buffs the carving enthusiastically with a bristle brush and rough burlap. The resultant carving resembles a well-worn folk art fish decoy that might be fifty years old.

"I'm more concerned with the overall patina, with creating an interesting object, than with making an accurate replica of a fish," he explains. "I like the shape of the brook trout, and I like the worn look of old duck and fish decoys. You can tell they had been used a great deal. They had a function and performed it well."

To achieve this aged and worn appearance, Bob uses a variety of techniques. After he carved the brook trout (featured in volume 1 of this series), he aged the wood with an acidic solution of vinegar, and then he applied dirty paint thinner and set the fish afire. After a buffing to remove charred wood, the cedar had a definite aged look.

The process of aging the wood is important because once Bob has painted the fish, he buffs off some of the paint and the wood will show through, and Bob likes the wood to look as though it had been in someone's barn loft for a century or so.

Bob paints the fish with Ronan brand Japan paints, thick, rich, concentrated colors often used in sign painting. Although the finished brook trout will not be especially colorful, a variety of paints are used. Some of the colors are muted and subtle, but their presence helps create a deep, rich finish.

In painting the brook trout, Bob will use Ronan Van Dyke brown, flake white, raw sienna, French yellow ochre, C. P. green dark, Prussian blue, and liberty red. Ronan paints are made by the T. J. Ronan Paint Corp., 749 E. 135th St., Bronx, NY 10454 and are available in building-supply and paint stores.

For information on Bob Swain's fish and bird carvings, write him at P.O. Box 1631, Parksley, VA 23421.

Bob begins by painting the belly of the brook trout with Ronan flake white tinted with small amounts of French yellow ochre and raw sienna, just enough to produce an off-white.

While the off-white is still wet, raw sienna is
applied to the sides of the fish and blended with
the off-white where the two colors meet.

Neatness is not mandatory at this stage. Bob allows the colors to overlap, creating a soft, gradual edge. The raw sienna is applied along the entire length of the fish.

Next, Bob paints the back of the fish with Van Dyke brown. The color is diluted somewhat with paint thinner.

C. P. green is applied below the brown and is blended into it. Bob likes the colors to merge gradually and share values. Again, this is not a precise technique, and one of the appealing things about it is that each fish has its own distinctive look.

Bob creates some subtle highlights in the fish by
applying raw sienna and liberty red. A small
amount of red is blended into the other colors
along the sides, and the raw sienna is applied to
the head.

The cheek area gets a little red highlight. If the highlights are too bright, they can be toned down with brown.

The basic paint job is completed. Notice how Bob has blended the colors to create areas of red, green, and raw sienna. Next he will age them through a careful application of heat.

While still wet, the oil-based paints are very flammable. Bob uses a kitchen match and carefully burns the paint. His shop has a concrete floor, and he performs this step well away from other flammable objects.

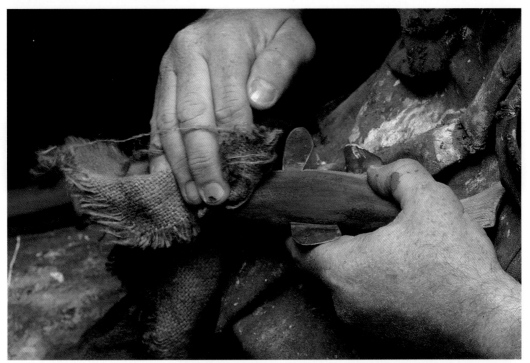

Burning helps dry the paints, and as soon as the
fish cools off, Bob buffs it with a piece of rough
burlap. This step removes burned and blistered
paint and allows the aged wood to show through.

A second buffing is done with a bristle brush. This gives a slight luster to the paint, as though the fish had been handled a great deal.

With the burning and buffing completed, Bob is ready to add detail. He begins with liberty red and a small brush, painting the gill covers and the mouth.

The eyes are thumbtacks whose paint has been removed. Bob repaints them with a mixture of Van Dyke brown, raw sienna, and liberty red, which results in a warm brown.

The leading edges of the pectoral, pelvic, and anal fins are painted off-white, the same mixture Bob used when painting the belly.

Van Dyke brown warmed with a little red is used to paint lines along the fins, suggesting spines.

Bob paints one bold line next to the white, and then adds several smaller lines to each fin.

Straight Van Dyke brown is used to add pupils to the eyes. This color stands out when applied over the warmer, lighter version.

The sides of the fish are detailed with small dots of color. Bob uses a wooden match to dab the color on. Here he begins with French yellow ochre darkened with a bit of brown.

Next Bob applies specks of Prussian blue lightened with white. Then he sharpens the match and applies tiny dots of red on about half of the blue specks.

Detailing is almost complete now. After the paint dries, Bob will buff the fish again with the bristle brush, and the boldness of the specks will be subdued.

The dots that appear along the sides of the fish become ''squiggles'' near the back. Bob applies these with raw sienna darkened with Van Dyke brown.

Van Dyke brown diluted with thinner is used to paint dark splotches on the tail fin and the dorsal fin.

The completed brook trout. All that remains is to buff the fish, a step that will mute the colors somewhat and give the finish a handsome luster.